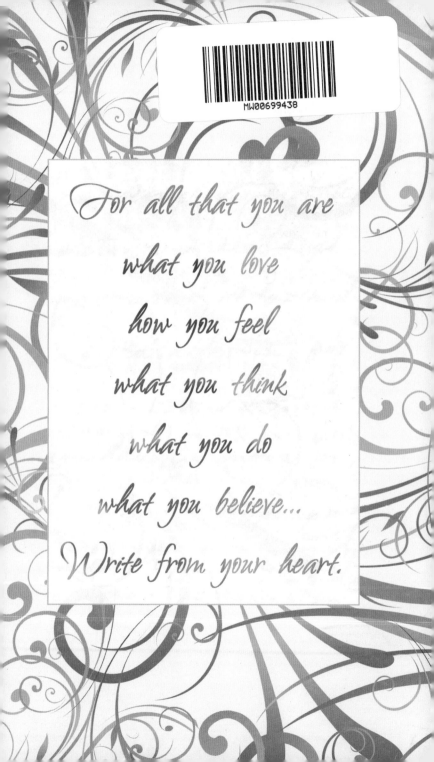

For all that you are
what you love
how you feel
what you think
what you do
what you believe...
Write from your heart.

Write

JOURNAL

Belle City Gifts
Savage, Minnesota, USA
Belle City Gifts is an imprint of BroadStreet Publishing Group LLC.
Broadstreetpublishing.com

Write JOURNAL

ISBN 978-1-4245-5616-8 (Spring Green)

Design by Chris Garborg | garborgdesign.com
Compiled and edited by Michelle Winger | literallyprecise.com

Printed in China.

18 19 20 21 22 23 24   7 6 5 4 3 2 1

We don't see ourselves as capable enough to do anything in our own strength,
for our true competence flows from God's empowering presence.

2 Corinthians 3:5

He will watch over his lovers,
never letting them slip or be overthrown.

Psalm 55:22

"All who come to me, I will embrace and will never turn them away."

John 6:37

He chose us to be his very own, joining us to himself
even before he laid the foundation of the universe!

Ephesians 1:4

You're the only place of protection for me. I keep coming back to hide myself in you, for you are like a mountain-cliff fortress where I am kept safe.

Respond gently when you are confronted
and you'll defuse the rage of another.

Proverbs 15:1

If anyone asks about the hope living within you,
always be ready to explain your faith with gentleness and respect.

"What blessing comes to you when gentleness lives in you!
For you will inherit the earth."

Matthew 5:5

"Don't worry or surrender to your fear.
For if you've believed in God, now trust and believe in me also."

John 14:1

Make all of this your constant meditation and make it real with your life
so everyone can see that you are moving forward.

1 Timothy 4:15

Pour out all your worries and stress upon him and leave them there,
for he always tenderly cares for you.

1 Peter 5:7

Surrender your anxiety!
Be silent and stop your striving and you will see that I am God.

Psalm 46:10

Be cheerful with joyous celebration in every season of life.
Let joy overflow, for you are united with the Anointed One!

Philippians 4:4

Everything we could ever need for life and complete devotion to God
has already been deposited in us by his divine power.

Faith, then, is birthed in a heart that responds
to God's anointed utterance of the Anointed One.

Romans 10:17

Watch your words and be careful what you say,
and you'll be surprised how few troubles you'll have.

Proverbs 21:23

Send your kind mercy-kiss to comfort me, your servant,
just like you promised you would.

Psalm 119:76

You are my only hope, Lord!
I've hung onto you, trusting in you all my life.

Psalm 71:5

Since we have this confidence, we can also have great boldness before him,
for if we present any request agreeable to his will, he will hear us.

1 John 5:14

We come freely and boldly to where love is enthroned, to receive mercy's kiss
and discover the grace we urgently need to strengthen us in our time of weakness.

Hebrews 4:16

Cheer up! Take courage all you who love him.
Wait for him to break through for you, all who trust in him!

Psalm 31:24

We constantly pray that our God will empower you
to live worthy of all that he has invited you to experience.

2 Thessalonians 1:11

Let gentleness be seen in every relationship, for our Lord is ever near.

Philippians 4:5

A man of deep understanding will give good advice,
drawing it out from the well within.

Brilliant ideas pay off and bring you prosperity,
but making hasty, impatient decisions will only lead to financial loss.

Proverbs 21:5

Put your heart and soul into every activity you do,
as though you are doing if for the Lord himself and not merely for others.

Colossians 3:23

All who seek you will see God do this for them. And they'll overflow with gladness.
Let this revive your hearts, all you lovers of God!

Psalm 69:32

Discover creative ways to encourage others and to motivate them
toward acts of compassion, doing beautiful works as expressions of love.

Hebrews 10:24

Faith brings our hopes into reality and becomes the foundation needed to acquire the things we long for. It is the evidence required to prove what is still unseen.

Hebrews 11:1

When we live our lives within the shadow of God Most High,
our secret hiding place, we will always be shielded from harm.

Psalm 91:9

"If you have faith inside of you no bigger than the size of a small mustard seed, you can say to this mountain, 'Move away from here and go over there,' and you will see it move."

Matthew 17:20

Love never brings fear, for fear is always related to punishment.
But love's perfection drives the fear of punishment far from our hearts.

1 John 4:18

God sends angels with special orders to protect you wherever you go,
defending you from all harm.

Psalm 91:11

Lord, you are so good to me, so kind in every way
and ready to forgive, for your grace-fountain keeps overflowing,
drenching all your lovers who pray to you.

Psalm 86:5

Farther than from a sunrise to a sunset—
that's how far you've removed our guilt from us.

Psalm 103:12

"If you embrace the truth, it will release more freedom into your lives."

John 8:32

The steps of the God-pursuing ones follow firmly in the footsteps of the Lord,
and God delights in every step they take to follow him.

Psalm 37:23

We are convinced that every detail of our lives is continually woven together
to fit into God's perfect plan of bringing good into our lives,
for we are his lovers who have been called to fulfill his designed purpose.

Romans 8:28

Within your heart you can make plans for your future,
but the Lord chooses the steps you take to get there.

Proverbs 16:9

Truthful words will stand the test of time,
but one day every lie will be seen for what it is.

In the midst of everything be always giving thanks,
for this is God's perfect plan for you in Christ Jesus.

1 Thessalonians 5:18

If anyone longs to be wise, ask God for wisdom and he will give it!

James 1:5

"When the truth-giving Spirit comes,
he will unveil the reality of every truth within you."

John 16:13

Let everyone thank God, for he is good, and he is easy to please!
His tender love for us continues on forever!

"I leave the gift of peace with you—my peace.
Not the kind of fragile peace given by the world, but my perfect peace.
Don't yield to fear or be troubled in your hearts—instead, be courageous!"

John 14:27

I know that you delight to set your truth deep in my spirit.
So come into the hidden places of my heart and teach me wisdom.

Psalm 51:6

"I will answer your cry for help every time you pray,
and you will find and feel my presence even in your time of pressure and trouble."

Psalm 91:15

May God, the inspiration and fountain of hope, fill you to overflowing
with uncontainable joy and perfect peace as you trust in him.

Romans 15:13

Laying your life down in tender surrender before the Lord
will bring life, prosperity, and honor as your reward.

Proverbs 22:4

Refusing constructive criticism shows you have no interest in improving your life.
For revelation-insight only comes as you accept correction
and the wisdom that it brings.

Proverbs 15:32

The Lord is my revelation-light to guide me along the way;
He's the source of my salvation to defend me every day. I fear no one!

Psalm 27:1

You draw near to those who call out to you,
listening closely, especially when their hearts are true.

Psalm 145:18

"Behold, I'm standing at the door, knocking. If your heart is open to hear my voice and you open the door within, I will come in to you and feast with you, and you will feast with me."

Revelation 3:20

"Never forget that I am with you every day, even to the completion of this age."

Matthew 28:20

If we freely admit our sins when his light uncovers them,
he will be faithful to forgive us every time.

1 John 1:9

Yes, he did mighty miracles and we are overjoyed!

Psalm 126:3

Don't be pulled in different directions or worried about a thing.
Be saturated in prayer throughout each day,
offering your faith-filled requests before God with overflowing gratitude.

Philippians 4:6

Let the sunrise of your love end our dark night. Break through our clouded dawn again!
Only you can satisfy our hearts, filling us with songs of joy to the end of our days.

Psalm 90:14

Through our faith, the mighty power of God constantly guards us
until our full salvation is ready to be revealed in the last time.

1 Peter 1:5

"You can ask and keep on asking him!
And you can be sure that you'll receive what you ask for,
and your joy will have no limits!"

John 16:24

Walk holy, in a way that is suitable to your high rank,
given to you in your divine calling.

Ephesians 4:1-2

Don't allow your hearts to grow dull or lose your enthusiasm,
but follow the example of those who fully received what God had promised
because of their strong faith and patient endurance.

Hebrews 6:12

"Everything I've taught you is so that the peace which is in me will be in you
and will give you great confidence as you rest in me."

John 16:33

This is the one who gives his strength and might to his people.
This is the Lord giving us his kiss of peace.

Psalm 29:11

We've kept you always in our prayers that you would receive
the perfect knowledge of God's pleasure over your lives.

Colossians 1:9

If your faith remains strong, even while surrounded by life's difficulties,
you will continue to experience the untold blessings of God!

James 1:12

Don't allow yourselves to be weary or disheartened in planting good seeds,
for the season of reaping the wonderful harvest you've planted is coming!

Galatians 6:9

When it seems as though you are facing nothing but difficulties,
see it as an invaluable opportunity to experience the greatest joy that you can!

James 1:2–3

"You will be satisfied with a full life and with all that I do for you.
For you will enjoy the fullness of my salvation!"

Psalm 91:16

Lord, I have chosen you alone as my inheritance.
You are my prize, my pleasure, and my portion.
I leave my destiny and its timing in your hands.

Psalm 16:5

The lovers of God who chase after righteousness will find all their dreams come true:
an abundant life drenched with favor and a fountain that overflows with satisfaction.

Proverbs 21:21

Don't lose your bold, courageous faith, for you are destined for a great reward!

Hebrews 10:35

Be assured that anything you do that is beautiful and excellent
will be repaid by our Lord, whether you are an employee or an employer.

Ephesians 6:8

Whom have I in heaven but you? You're all I want!
No one on earth means as much to me as you.

Psalm 73:25

Lord, so many times I fail; I fall into disgrace. But when I trust in you, I have a strong and glorious presence protecting and anointing me. Forever you're all I need!

Psalm 73:26

Praise God for his astonishing gift, which is far too great for words!

2 Corinthians 9:15

Let your heart always be guided by the peace of the Anointed One,
who called you to peace as part of his one body. And always be thankful.

Colossians 3:15

The wisdom from above is always pure, filled with peace, considerate and teachable.
It is filled with love and never displays prejudice or hypocrisy in any form.

James 3:17

"Does worry add anything to your life?
Can it add one more year, or even one day?"

Luke 12:25